Peter a poet
and lyracist
Truth Seeker
a follower of the
PRINCE OF Peace
HUMBLAY Hombray
Peter
GILSON
692-0908

One-Minute Praises

STEVE MILLER

HARVEST HOUSE PUBLISHERS
EUGENE, OREGON

Cover by Terry Dugan Design, Minneapolis, Minnesota

Cover photo © Harrison Eastwood / Digital Vision / Getty Images

Emphasis in Scripture quotations is added by the author.

ONE-MINUTE PRAISES
Copyright © 2006 by Steve Miller
Published by Harvest House Publishers
Eugene, Oregon 97402

ISBN-13: 978-0-7369-1788-9
ISBN-10: 0-7369-1788-8
Product # 6917889

Printed in the United States of America

06 07 08 09 10 11 12 / BP-CF / 10 9 8 7 6 5 4 3 2

From the rising of the sun to its going down
the LORD's name is to be praised.

PSALM 113:3

With heartfelt thanks to the prayer team.
Together we have seen God work in mighty ways.

Contents

Before You Begin

∽

Praise is one of the most uplifting and encouraging activities we can engage in as Christians. No prayer is complete without words of praise, and no day is complete without expressions of praise.

To praise God means to worship Him and give thanks to Him. It is to recognize who He is and what He has done, to enhance His reputation, and to express gratefulness to Him.

The psalmist wrote, "I will bless the LORD at all times; His praise shall continually be in my mouth" (Psalm 34:1). Praising God continually through the day may at first seem a challenge, but you'll discover that the more you deliberately look around you for reasons to worship and thank God, the more praise will become a habit—one that you will come to enjoy because it increases your awareness of Him, deepens your appreciation for Him, and thus draws you closer to Him.

So as you read through the one-minute praises in this book, rather than simply stop at the end of each reading, allow each page to serve as a "starter" for you—a starter that helps begin your day on a note of praise that continues throughout the day.

At times, of course, praising God is not easy. When life gets painful and our hearts are discouraged, lifting our voices in worship can be difficult. Yet the apostle Paul lovingly exhorts us to be "giving thanks *always* for *all* things to God" (Ephesians 5:20)—and that includes the trials of life. Praising God is easy when all is well. But God's desire is for our joy to be based not on our circumstances but on who He is and what He can do for us. The most beautiful and heartfelt praise is that which, in the midst of suffering, can say, "Lord, even though everything is going wrong I know You are good and will take care of me."

This kind of abandonment and trust brings us to the end of our resources and to full dependence upon God's. This is what nurtures stronger faith—the kind in which we yield ourselves and our situations to God so He can bring us to greater spiritual maturity.

As you journey through this book, may you discover many new reasons to praise God—and may praise become a richer and more meaningful part of your life.

God's Greatness

O worship the King, all glorious above,
O gratefully sing His power and His love;
Our Shield and Defender, the Ancient of Days,
Pavilioned in splendor and girded with praise.

SIR ROBERT H. GRANT
"O WORSHIP THE KING"

Great Thoughts
About a Great God

Great is our Lord, and mighty in power;
His understanding is infinite.

PSALM 147:5

☙

Father, how very *great* You are! You are beyond comprehension and measure. Even with all that You have revealed about Yourself in the Bible, so much about You will always be beyond my understanding.

Help me to avoid the mistake of reducing You to someone or something You are not. May I never limit You by thinking of You in human terms. My heart's desire is to lift up and honor You by always recognizing that You are "able to do exceedingly abundantly above all that we ask or think" (Ephesians 3:20).

May my every thought of You always exalt You!

A Worthy View of God

You, whose name alone is the LORD,
are the Most High over all the earth.

PSALM 83:18

༄

Nothing is above You, O Lord. You are the highest above all. You are the Supreme Ruler over all kings, kingdoms, and thrones. Everything that dwells in this universe is subject to Your authority and command.

My limited human mind cannot comprehend how infinitely great You are. And I am humbled that You, the Most High over all the heavens, have lovingly reached down to the dust of the earth to show grace, compassion, and mercy to me.

Though You have chosen to lower Yourself to walk with me, may I never lower my thoughts of You. May I never lose my sense of Your awesome majesty. May I always elevate my thoughts of You so that they are more and more worthy of You.

Incomprehensible Greatness

*Great is the LORD, and greatly to be praised;
and His greatness is unsearchable.*

PSALM 145:3

∽

Lord, I could never fathom the height, depth, length, and breadth of Your greatness. As I think about all that is true about You, I am moved to the depths of humility and the heights of praise.

In Your perfect wisdom, You never make a mistake. In Your perfect power, You are never defeated. In Your perfect knowledge, You are never wrong or unaware. In Your perfect faithfulness, You never break a promise. In Your perfect love, You are never unkind. In Your perfect holiness, You never sin. In Your perfect justice, You are never unfair.

I could say so much more…yet words could never suffice. I am so awed, I can only bow down before You in silent worship. Help me to be still and know that You are God.

God's Sovereignty

Even to discuss the authority of Almighty God seems
a bit meaningless, and to question it would be absurd.
Can we imagine the Lord God of Hosts
having to request permission of anyone or
to apply for anything to a higher body?
To whom would God go for permission?
Who is higher than the Highest?
Who is mightier than the Almighty?
Whose position antedates that of the Eternal?
At whose throne would God kneel?
Where is the greater one to whom He must appeal?[1]

A.W. TOZER

It's All from Him

The earth is the LORD's, and all its fullness,
the world and those who dwell therein.

PSALM 24:1

❧

Heavenly Father, thank You for the psalmist's affirmation that the earth is Yours—all of it. You *created* it out of nothing. You *sustain* it with a power too great for me to understand. You *govern* its ongoings according to Your perfect plans. And You *provide* for all the needs of Your creation through the resources of the land, sky, and sea.

I am richly blessed, Father, by the abundance You've placed all around me. Sometimes I don't notice it because I'm so busy or because I'm so preoccupied with the things that come from human hands rather than Your divine hands. Help me to always have a right perspective…and to begin and end every one of my days by acknowledging that ultimately, everything I have comes from You.

Achieving His Grand Purpose

Whatever the Lord pleases He does,
in heaven and in earth,
in the seas and in all deep places.

PSALM 135:6

∾

I thank You, Lord, for the Bible's many reminders of Your complete power over all things. This truth is a source of comfort for me when I see the wicked attempt to somehow thwart Your plans. I admit that sometimes I'm tempted to believe You cannot anticipate their actions, and the best You can do is minimize the damage left in their wake.

But Your Word says otherwise. No corner of the earth is so remote, no living soul so rebellious that it can act separately from Your sovereignty. You have the power to orchestrate the affairs of men, nations, and even the natural world so that they achieve Your grand purpose. Whatever You please to do *will* happen. For that I praise Your name!

Nothing Can Overrule
God's Plan

*Heaven and the highest heavens belong to the LORD
your God, also the earth with all that is in it.*

DEUTERONOMY 10:14

~

Lord, thank You for the security and comfort that
comes from knowing You are sovereign over all heaven and
earth. Sometimes I get frustrated because the world seems
so out of control or because I don't understand why You
allow bad things to happen. Help me to not despair over
what I don't understand, but instead, to trust in what the
Bible says about You—that the earth and heavens belong
to You.

Because of this truth, I can have full confidence that
everything You plan *will* come to pass. That You *will* prevail
over those who oppose You and Your children. That You
will wipe away all sin and sorrow. And that You *will* set
up Your perfect and glorious kingdom, which *will* last
forever and ever.

A Sovereignty We Can Trust

Yours, O LORD, is the greatness,
the power and the glory,
the victory and the majesty;
for all that is in heaven and earth is Yours…
and You are exalted as head over all.

1 CHRONICLES 29:11

∽

Heavenly Father, Your sovereignty has no limits. Words are not adequate to describe the extent of Your rule over the universe. Your throne had no beginning and will have no end. You are all-powerful over all things at all times. No greatness is higher than Yours.

Because You are in full control of all that is in heaven and earth, I can rest assured You are also in full control of every detail of my life. Nothing will happen to me without Your permission. Though I may not understand why some things come my way, I can trust that You have a purpose and that no person will overrule You. How comforting it is to know I will never be exposed to anything that is beyond Your control! Yours is a sovereignty I can trust.

More Than Adequate

I know that You can do everything,
and that no purpose of Yours
can be withheld from You.

JOB 42:2

∽

Lord, my human perspective is so limited. Just because something looks impossible to me doesn't mean it's impossible to You. Just because I cannot see the answer doesn't mean You lack one.

You are sovereign, so I know You are supreme over every circumstance in my life regardless of how severe it is. Your good purpose will always win out. You will never be defeated…and consequently, neither will I. Help me to not become distraught by temporary tribulation but to be calmed by Your permanent providence.

Thank You, Father, that I can rest on the bedrock of Your sovereignty even in the harshest of life's storms. Your power is far more than adequate to handle my every need!

Supreme over All

In Your hand is there not power and might,
so that no one is able to withstand You?

2 CHRONICLES 20:6

❧

Lord of all, every single one of Your decrees have been or will be fulfilled. Every person and every creature on this earth—willingly or unwillingly—is as wet clay on Your potter's wheel. You are able to use even the plots of Your enemies to accomplish whatever You please.

I praise You that Your power is so great none can defy it, Your throne is so high none can overthrow it, and Your counsel is so established none can change it.

That You are supreme over all gives me great security—for it means nothing can happen to me apart from Your plans, nothing can deprive me of Your promises, and nothing can interrupt Your provision from flowing to me.

Lord of the Possible

Oh, give thanks to the LORD! Call upon His name;
make known His deeds among the peoples!

PSALM 105:1

∽

Lord, from a human perspective, it should have been impossible to create something out of nothing. For the whole earth to be covered by a flood. For the Red Sea to part and close up again. For mere shouts and trumpets to fell the walls of Jericho. For Gideon's 300 to defeat an enemy of thousands upon thousands. For Daniel to survive a lions' den, and for his friends to walk unscathed in a fiery furnace. For a virgin to give birth. For the Lord Jesus to heal multitudes, walk on water, and rise from the dead to forever conquer death. And for me who was dead in sin to become alive in Christ.

Yet You have accomplished every one of these mighty deeds...and more. Whenever I doubt You, Lord, remind me of Your great works. You are the Lord of the possible!

God's Faithfulness

Far above all finite comprehension
is the unchanging faithfulness of God.
Everything about God is great, vast,
incomparable. He never forgets, never fails,
never falters, never forfeits His word.[2]

A.W. PINK

Always Faithful

Has God forgotten to be gracious?
Has He in anger shut up His tender mercies?...
I will remember the works of the LORD;
surely I will remember Your wonders of old.

PSALM 77:9-11

∾

Father, sometimes I struggle and wonder if You've forgotten me. When I consider my circumstances, I see problems that remain unsolved. I feel as if, for some reason, You aren't at work in my life. I've even doubted Your love and care.

Yet I know Your track record of faithfulness. When I look back, I can remember those so very clear times You rescued me. Those times when You gave me a blessing greater than I ever expected. Those times when You answered my prayers in the most powerful way.

When life isn't going so well, help me to remember Your mighty deeds and wonders of old. They're written all over the Bible, and they're written on the tablet of my life. And may the confidence I receive from what You've done in the past give me renewed courage for the future.

He Is Able

There is nothing too hard for You.

JEREMIAH 32:17

✍

Heavenly Father, Your faithfulness and sovereignty amaze me.

Whatever You start, You finish. Whatever You promise, You fulfill. No problem is too great for You to handle; no circumstance is beyond Your control.

The knowledge that nothing can derail Your plans and promises for me is a source of great comfort—especially as I struggle against my human weaknesses and failings. As Philippians 1:6 says, I can be confident that the work You began in me *will* be carried on to completion. I praise You that one day, my struggles will be no more. I will have a glorified body and dwell with You in heaven forever and ever...all because You are faithful.

Every Promise Kept

There has not failed one word of all His good promise.

1 KINGS 8:56

✺

Father, I praise You that Your promises never fail. You always keep Your word, as the pages of Scripture make clear. The evidence of Your faithfulness is overwhelming.

And yet when I consider Your promises to me, I admit sometimes I become anxious. When You don't seem to be meeting my needs or answering my prayers, I get impatient, wondering when You're going to come to my rescue.

Help me to remember that in the Bible, some promises weren't fulfilled for months, years, and even centuries. Yet You have always fulfilled Your perfect plan in Your perfect time. I praise You for teaching me to wait…so that my confidence in You may grow stronger than ever.

Forever the Same

I am the LORD, I do not change....

MALACHI 3:6

∽

You are always faithful, even when I go astray. You are always wise, even when I question You. You are always in control, even when I defy Your will.

You are always attentive, even when I'm not listening. You are always just, even when I feel You're unfair. You are always seeking my best, even when I'm at my worst.

I praise You for always loving me, even when I am uncaring. I praise You for always pursuing me, even when I am unworthy. And I praise You for always being You, regardless of what I do.

God's Goodness

God only is infinitely good. A boundless goodness
that knows no limits, a goodness as infinite as his essence,
not only good, but best; not only good, but goodness itself,
the supreme inconceivable goodness.[3]

STEPHEN CHARNOCK

An Enduring Goodness

The LORD is good;
His mercy is everlasting,
and His truth endures to all generations.

PSALM 100:5

✑

Thank You, Lord, for the Bible's many assurances of Your goodness. In the times when I am tempted to question You, may I remember that Your goodness is absolutely perfect in every way. It is a goodness that does not make mistakes, and it is a goodness that emanates from every part of Your nature. It's who You are!

And I praise You that Your mercies are everlasting. They will never run dry; they will never be revoked. The mercies You poured out on the great men and women of the Bible are the same mercies I can count on today…and tomorrow and forever.

Your goodness and mercies, O Lord, fill me with a warm sense of security. Yes, great is Your faithfulness!

God Is Good

Give thanks to the LORD, for He is good!
For His mercy endures forever.

PSALM 107:1

✍

Lord, Your Word says repeatedly that You are good. I know that's true because of the evidence I've seen in my life. And yet sometimes the dark clouds of tragedy or pain hinder my ability to see Your goodness.

What about horrible disasters that take many lives? What about terrible injustices in which people are grievously wronged? And what about the losses, hurts, and disappointments in my own life that don't seem to make sense?

At times like these, I need to remember that You are God, and I'm not. The hard questions of life are not mine to answer but Yours. I praise You that regardless of what happens, I can know with certainty that You *are* good.

His Many Benefits

Taste and see that the LORD is good....

PSALM 34:8

❧

How great, O Father, is Your goodness! I cannot comprehend its immensity. Nor do I always recognize it for what it is. Yet may I always acknowledge Your favor and kindness upon me. May I always praise You for every benefit You have given me, regardless of how small.

Because of Your goodness, You continue to give me life and breath. You continue to bless me with spiritual riches and eternal hope. You continue to provide for my every need and preserve me in my every circumstance.

Where, O Lord, would I be without Your favor? Your Word says that every good thing I have in life is from You (James 1:17). May my heart treasure every good gift You have given to me, and may everything I do today magnify Your goodness.

His Goodness Is Unchanging

Oh, give thanks to the LORD, for He is good!
PSALM 106:1

❧

Your goodness, dear Lord, is the fountain from which all blessings flow. It is spontaneous and generous; it is perfect and eternal. It cannot be earned; neither can it be repaid. So abundant is Your goodness that You make the sun to shine on the unrighteous as well as the righteous and send the rain to pour on the unjust as well as the just. Your goodness is evident in everything You do, from the outpouring of Your love to the exercising of Your justice.

When I am tempted to doubt Your goodness, remind me that it is unchanging. Teach me to look for Your goodness even when I am overwhelmed by sorrow and tribulation. And help me to rest in Your faithfulness, which assures me that Your goodness will always endure.

The Magnitude of His Blessings

Blessed be the Lord,
who daily loads us with benefits,
the God of our salvation!

PSALM 68:19

∽

Lord, who am I that You have favored me so greatly? You have made me in Your image, given me the breath of life, and made possible my salvation so that I may enjoy a personal relationship with You.

You have surrounded me with the majestic splendor of the heavens and the earth. Every day, I see and experience new testimonies to Your creativity, power, and wisdom. You have filled the world with good things for my pleasure and my provision.

I am filled with admiration at the magnitude of Your goodness to me. With each new morning, may I look around me afresh and determine to fully savor every blessing I receive from Your hand. May I never fail to praise You for all You've given to me.

God's Love

*As Christians...we ought to see that everything we enjoy in
life—from our tiniest pleasures to the eternal redemption
we have found in Christ—is an expression of the great love
wherewith God loved us. The blessing of His love comes to
us not because we deserve it, but simply and only because of
His sovereign grace....In light of the glories of divine love,
how can we not be utterly lost in wonder, love, and praise?*

JOHN MACARTHUR

An Inexhaustible Love

I will cry out to God Most High,
to God who performs all things for me.

PSALM 57:2

✀

I am both awed and humbled, Lord, when I consider that You are God Most High, and yet You involve Yourself so intimately in my life. You are never too busy for me, and none of my concerns are too insignificant for You.

You are my Rock, my Fortress, my Shepherd. You are my Friend, my Champion, my Deliverer. You delight in me as Your child, lavish Your love on me, and guide me through every circumstance. Though You are ruler over all the universe, Your care for me is so complete it's as if nothing else existed. Yes, You are a God "who performs all things for me."

Thank You that I cannot exhaust all the ways You express Your care. How precious to me is Your love!

His Perfect Love for Us

*Behold what manner of love the Father has
bestowed on us, that we should be called
children of God!*

1 JOHN 3:1

∽

Lord, I praise You that Your love for me has no limits.
It's a love that cares for me in spite of all my shortcomings.
You love me because You *want* to, not because You *have* to.
And You are faithful to show Your love to me even when
I'm not faithful to You.

Your love is a perfect love—it is...

a love that is consistent,
a love that is constant,
a love that is complete.

Your perfect love knows exactly what I need and when
I need it...whether it be encouragement, guidance, or
even correction. And it is a love that has chosen to make
me Your child. How generous, how magnificent, how
indescribable is Your love!

A Many-Splendored Love

*You, O Lord, are a God full of compassion, and gracious,
longsuffering and abundant in mercy and truth.*

PSALM 86:15

❧

Heavenly Father, Your love for me is manifest in so
many ways!

Your compassion comforts me in the midst of my
hurts and weaknesses. Your grace redeems me from
condemnation and showers me with blessings though I do
not deserve them. Your longsuffering is a divine patience
that never gives up on me when I question or fail You. Your
mercy chooses to forgive my sin and make me a citizen of
heaven. And Your truth guides me and gives me wisdom
and hope for all the days of my life.

I am lost in wonder when I consider the immensity of
Your love for me. It will stand forever and never cease to
be. May I bring more praise to You by letting Your many-
splendored love shine through my life to others.

A Love Without Parallel

*God demonstrates His own love toward us, in that
while we were still sinners, Christ died for us.*

ROMANS 5:8

❧

Father, of all the praises I could ever sing to You,
surely the greatest by far is praise for what Your Son did
on the cross. There the world can see the most glorious
display of divine love human eyes have ever witnessed.
Yours is a love without parallel, a love undeserved, a love
stronger than death.

How brightly did Your love shine as Jesus bled on the
cross—as He endured the brutal nails, the piercing thorns,
the excruciating pain! I should have paid the price, and
yet Your Son graciously took my place and endured the
fullness of Your wrath.

I am humbled, Lord, by the greatness of Your love for
me. May every single day of my life be filled to overflowing
with gratitude and adoration for You.

Infinite Love

In this is love, not that we loved God, but that He loved us and sent His Son....

1 JOHN 4:10

✍

Father, it was Jesus' infinite love that led Him to kneel in agony and pray, "Not as I will, but as You will." It was His infinite love that led Him to endure betrayal, arrest, and injustice. It was His infinite love that enabled Him to bear the cruel scourging and the indescribable horrors of the crucifixion.

Because He took on my sin, I can one day be holy. Because He was willing to die on the cross, I can one day live in Your kingdom. And because He wore a crown of thorns, I can one day wear a crown of glory.

Thank You, Father, for all that Your Son's love has accomplished. It is a love too great to fathom, a love for which I could never give enough thanks. May His infinite love for me inspire infinite praise from me!

God's Mercy

When all Thy mercies, O my God,
My rising soul surveys,
Transported with the view, I'm lost
In wonder, love and praise.
Unnumbered comforts to my soul
Thy tender care bestowed
Before my infant heart conceived
From whom those comforts flowed.

JOSEPH ADDISON
"WHEN ALL THY MERCIES, O MY GOD"

Rejoicing in His Mercy

For as the heavens are high above the earth,
so great is His mercy toward those who fear Him.

PSALM 103:11

❧

Father, I praise You for Your incredible mercy. As I look back on the times I have failed You, I realize You have given me second chances, third chances, and more. When I have stumbled and succumbed to temptation, You have stood nearby, ready to pick me up. When I have asked forgiveness for my trespasses, You have lavished it upon me freely.

I am humbled when I consider the extent of Your mercy. It burst forth as a fountain when You chose to save me in eternity past and will flow as a steady stream all the way into eternity future. Your mercy is new every morning and blesses me all the day long. Because of Your mercy, Lord, I have confidence for today and hope for tomorrow!

Abundant in Mercy

You, Lord, are good, and ready to forgive,
and abundant in mercy to all those who call upon You.

PSALM 86:5

∽

My heart rejoices over Your goodness to me, Lord. When I confess my sin, You are ready to forgive. Your mercies are constant, and Your compassions are new every morning.

Though at times I slip and fall, You are patient with me. With tenderness You pick me up and restore me. With lovingkindness You come alongside me and instruct me in the ways of righteousness.

Lord, I long for my life to be pleasing to You. And I praise You that I am not left to do this in my own power. You have been generous beyond what I could ever expect, and You have given me every resource I need. Thank You for Your incredible mercy!

God's Kindness

O God, I cannot number, I cannot express by words,
all the instances of thy fatherly kindness.
But so long as I live I will boast of thy grace,
and prolong in eternity that thanksgiving
which I have here so imperfectly begun.[5]

CHRISTOPHER CHRISTIAN STURM

Remembering His Kindness

*I will mention the lovingkindnesses of the LORD
and the praises of the LORD, according to all that
the LORD has bestowed on us.*

ISAIAH 63:7

∾

Father, help me not forget the many ways You've shown Your love for me. Your kindness to me began even before the foundation of the world, when You chose me to receive the gifts of salvation and eternal life. And Your goodness continues to be manifest in the ways You provide for all my physical and spiritual needs.

When I preoccupy myself with anxieties about the future, I easily lose sight of Your kindness in the past. Refresh my mind and heart with reminders of Your faithfulness. May the many lights of Your past kindnesses shine their rays forward and melt away the darkness and uncertainty that cover the path before me.

Above all, may my lips proclaim and praise Your kind acts so that others, too, may see how great You are.

Secure in His Kindness

The mountains shall depart and the hills be removed,
but My kindness shall not depart from you....

ISAIAH 54:10

❧

Father, You care for me as no one else can. You know my needs better than I do. While I cannot see past today's crises and circumstances, You can see all my tomorrows, and You are able to bring about the ultimate good that I have yet to understand.

I admit that when I'm faced with troubles and uncertainty, resting completely in Your loving and sovereign hands is hard for me. In my mind I know You are faithful, but in my heart I still struggle with fear.

Thank You for the promise that Your kindness will never depart from me. Because You are in control and You care, I have no reason to be afraid. May I always rest secure in You!

A Fount of Blessing

*What shall I render to the LORD
for all His benefits toward me?*

PSALM 116:12

∽

I love You, Lord, for giving me another day in which to experience Your kindness and grace. Every new morning is another gift from You, another opportunity to watch for the many mercies You send my way.

I can easily lose sight of the evidences of Your kindness in my life. Help me to watch for even the tiniest of blessings…in my family and friendships, in my work, in my home, in my church, and even in my meals and rest and play. And as I recognize Your gifts to me, may I immediately lift up praise to You, knowing that every good thing comes from Your hand.

You hold power over all my life; may I never take a single day or a single act of Your kindness for granted. What a fount of blessing You are to me!

Chosen for His Work

*To each one is given the manifestation of the
Spirit for the common good.*

1 CORINTHIANS 12:7 NASB

✑

Lord, Your kindness and generosity never cease to
amaze me. Not only have You saved me and are You
changing me, but You have also gifted me to fulfill a
needed role in Your church. With perfect foresight, You
knew exactly where I could be of greatest use...for the
good of others in the body of Christ.

I thank You that no Christian is a mere spectator and
that all are participants. You've placed me among fellow
believers who can minister to me as I minister to them. I
marvel at how You have interwoven all our lives so that
when we work together, individual needs are met and the
whole church is built up.

I know You don't need me to help do Your work on
earth, Lord...yet You've chosen to work through me. What
a gracious God You are!

God's Care

Come, Thou Fount of every blessing,
Tune my heart to sing Thy grace;
Streams of mercy, never ceasing,
Call for songs of loudest praise.
Teach me some melodious sonnet,
Sung by flaming tongues above;
Praise His name! I'm fixed upon it!
Name of God's redeeming love.

ROBERT ROBINSON
"COME, THOU FOUNT"

Always Watching

*The eyes of the LORD are on the righteous,
and His ears are open to their cry.*

PSALM 34:15

❧

Father, You watch over me every day and every night without ceasing. All Your thoughts about me are thoughts of fatherly love and concern.

Your eyes are so attentively focused on me, I know I have no reason to fear my safety. Your arms are protectively folded around me as if I were Your one and only child. Your ears are so alert to my cries for help, I know You will always intercede in times of trouble.

Because of Your watchfulness, I have no reason to be anxious. To fret and worry would be to doubt and dishonor You. All through the ages You have never failed to care for any of Your own, and I know You will never fail to care for me. Thank You that I can always count on Your faithfulness!

A Solid Rock

He…set my feet upon a rock,
and established my steps.

PSALM 40:2

❧

Lord, if I can always count on anyone or anything, it's You and Your care. People will let me down, but You won't. Circumstances will cause me to slip and fall, but You are faithful to pick me up and place me where I can stand firm.

Remind me to always place my confidence not in myself but in You. You alone are the solid ground, the firm foundation upon which I need to place my life. And You alone are able to lift me up and establish me on the sure and everlasting rock of Your protection and peace.

Should I ever begin to place confidence in myself, help me to recognize it and relinquish it to You. Whatever happens in my life, Lord, I want it to be the result of Your divine accomplishment and not my human achievement.

A Guide We Can Trust

Trust in the LORD with all your heart,
and lean not on your own understanding;
in all your ways acknowledge Him,
and He shall direct your paths.

PROVERBS 3:5-6

❧

Thank You, Lord, that I don't have to figure out everything on my own. Sometimes life feels so out of control, and I'm not sure what I should do next. All around me, I hear the message that I need to be self-sufficient. But I know that doesn't really work—and that when I fail to consult You, I tend to mess things up.

Thank You that I can turn to You for guidance at any time. You are more than delighted to teach me, enlighten me, and lead me in the way I should go. You promise that if I place my full trust in You, You *will* direct my path.

Help me to rest in You and let You manage my life. I know that when I do, I won't feel so stressed or anxious.

All This and More

I will call upon the LORD, who is worthy to be praised.

2 SAMUEL 22:4

∽

Heavenly Father, whenever doubt creeps into my heart and I begin to question Your care for me, help me to remember...

Regardless of the temptations I face, You have provided a way of escape. Even when my sin is great, Your love and forgiveness are greater. As much as I may waver, Your faithfulness is firm as ever. Regardless of how destitute I may feel, You will always provide for me. As high as the mountain before me may rise, You are higher still. Regardless of what attempts to hinder my relationship with You, nothing can separate me from Your love.

In every way, Father, You are higher...deeper...and greater. In every way You will sustain me, and You are worthy of unceasing praise!

Trusting, Leaning, and Praising

Hear my cry, O God; attend to my prayer....
When my heart is overwhelmed;
lead me to the rock that is higher than I.

PSALM 61:1-2

∽

Father, help me to recognize that true happiness comes only when I surrender all my concerns to You. Help me to remember that true relief comes only when I place all my burdens in Your hands. Teach me, O Lord, when sorrows surround me, not to seek their removal but to let Your will be done.

This is my heart's desire, Lord, because I want to lean not on my own might but Yours. Not on my own wisdom but Yours. And not on my own plans but Yours.

Lord, I want You to be my everything. I realize that until You are my all, I actually have nothing. Help me to trust You more, lean on You more, and above all, praise You more.

Always Alert

He who keeps you will not slumber.

PSALM 121:3

∽

Lord, You are my Keeper, my Protector, my Shepherd. Your watchfulness over me is constant and will never cease. You never grow tired; Your eyes never close. Though You rule over all the universe, the magnitude of Your work never fatigues You.

Because You are always alert, I have nothing to fear. No intruder—whether an enemy or a temptation—will ever catch You by surprise. Though the path of life may be dangerous and difficult at times, You will preserve me. As the psalmist said, "Even though I walk through the valley of the shadow of death, I will fear no evil, for you are with me" (Psalm 23:4 NIV).

Because You are always alert, I am able to rest. I am able to lie down in green pastures and beside still waters. Thank You, Lord, for the security Your attentive care gives to me.

A Patient Father

Gracious is the LORD, and righteous;
yes, our God is merciful.

PSALM 116:5

∽

Father, I sometimes don't learn very well, do I? I wouldn't be surprised if You're frustrated with me. I've fallen into this temptation before. And the blame is all mine. You promised a way of escape, and I didn't take it.

I thank You that You will never give up on me. How gentle Your longsuffering, how tender Your patience. Though I plunge into sin, You reach out to lift me up. In Your kindness, You are willing to restore me. Shouldn't I have learned this lesson already?

I marvel at Your patience, Father. May I never abuse it through deliberate disobedience. Convict me, and may I cry out to You for the strength and the will to choose the way of holiness.

God's Holiness

Holy, Holy, Holy! Though the darkness hide Thee,
Though the eye of sinful man Thy glory may not see,
Only Thou art Holy; there is none beside Thee
Perfect in power, in love, and purity.

REGINALD HEBER
"HOLY, HOLY, HOLY"

An Absolute Holiness

Exalt the LORD our God,
and worship at His holy hill;
for the LORD our God is holy.

PSALM 99:9

❧

Father, Your holiness is too great for me to fathom. It is so perfect, so pure, so unapproachable. It is so all-encompassing that all Your attributes are holy. Your wisdom is holy, Your love is holy, Your justice is holy, Your power is holy…everything about You is holy and therefore is worthy of praise!

In light of Your absolute holiness, I realize You cannot allow sin in Your presence. Illuminate my mind and direct my will so that I may resist temptation. Prompt me to flee from anything that would hinder my fellowship with You and soil my service to You. May my fear of Your holiness come from a reverence that desires to please You and a love that is determined not to grieve You. Remind me that when I am holy, I bring honor and glory to You.

The Benefits of His Holiness

Holy, holy, holy is the LORD of hosts;
The whole earth is full of His glory!

ISAIAH 6:3

∽

Lord, how beautiful is Your holiness! Every word You say and every work You do is perfect, pure, and undefiled. Every one of Your laws and judgments is altogether righteous. No trace of wrong or evil is in You.

Help me to never take Your holiness for granted. Without it, the cross and my salvation would have been impossible. I would be forever imprisoned in the dungeon of sin and darkness. Because of Your holiness, I am now free to enjoy the light of Your glory and grace.

And because You are holy, I know You will always deal with me truthfully, rightly, and fairly. Though I cannot always trust people, I know I can always trust You. I praise and thank You for what Your holiness means to me.

God's Knowledge

God perfectly knows Himself and,
being the source and author of all things,
it follows that He knows all that can be known.
And this He knows instantly and with a fullness
of perfection that includes every possible item
of knowledge concerning everything that exists
or could have existed anywhere in the universe
at any time in the past or that may exist
in the centuries or ages yet unborn.[6]

A.W. TOZER

Resting in His Perfect Knowledge

Oh, the depth of the riches both of the wisdom and knowledge of God! How unsearchable are His judgments and His ways past finding out!

ROMANS 11:33

∽

Father, You know everything. Nothing is hidden from You, and You have a perfect knowledge of the future.

This gives me *security,* because I know nothing will ever happen that takes You by surprise.

This gives me *peace,* because I know I can always turn to You when I don't have the answers.

This gives me *confidence,* because I know whatever You say will happen really *will* happen.

This gives me *comfort,* because I know You can see all my tomorrows, and You will lead me through them.

Thank You, Father, that Your perfect knowledge of all things can serve, for me, as a source of perfect peace in all things.

He Knows Us Well

You know my sitting down and my rising up;
You understand my thought afar off.
You comprehend my path and my lying down,
and are acquainted with all my ways.

PSALM 139:2-3

∽

Dear Lord, nothing in my life escapes Your notice, and You never forget anything. You have known me from before time began, and You know me better than I know myself.

Because You know everything perfectly, You know my every need and are able to take perfect care of me. You understand my every frailty and are able to provide perfect help for me. You know my every thought and are able to provide perfect counsel to me—whether it be conviction, direction, or encouragement.

That You know me so well gives me great comfort, Lord. That Your knowledge is perfect makes You a perfect Father and Friend for me.

God's Creative Power

All Thy works with joy surround Thee,
Earth and heaven reflect Thy rays,
Stars and angels sing around Thee,
Center of unbroken praise;
Field and forest, vale and mountain,
Flowering meadow, flashing sea,
Chanting bird and flowing fountain,
Call us to rejoice in Thee.

HENRY J. VAN DYKE
"JOYFUL, JOYFUL, WE ADORE THEE"

A Testimony of His Power

The heavens declare the glory of God;
and the firmament shows His handiwork.

PSALM 19:1

∽

Day and night, Father, I am reminded of how great You are. Every one of the heavenly bodies—the sun by day, and the planets and stars by night—moves with astounding mathematical precision and reliability. Their perfect order is a silent yet profound testimony of Your complete power over all the universe.

I praise You that Your greatness is so clearly manifest all around me, for it wonderfully reminds me, at all times, of what You can do. May the beauty and order of the heavens inspire within me a deeper trust and confidence in You—a confidence that realizes that if You are in full control of the universe, surely You are in full control of my life.

How Marvelous His Works!

You formed my inward parts;
You covered me in my mother's womb.
I will praise You, for I am
fearfully and wonderfully made....

PSALM 139:13-14

∽

Father, when I think about the incredible complexity and design of the human body, I never cease to be amazed. And the more that science learns, the more we realize how little we really know. Our bodies are awesome testimonies of the infinite greatness of Your wisdom and creativity.

I am especially in awe of the way my body sustains itself. My heartbeat, my breathing, and so many other processes continue to carry on without any effort on my part. Billions of cells are at work in a marvelous harmony that keeps me functioning...even when I am asleep!

I magnify You, Lord, for I am fearfully and wonderfully made. May I always honor Your handiwork by taking good care of what You've given me.

God's Greatness on Display

Praise Him, sun and moon;
praise Him, all you stars of light!
Praise Him, you heavens of heavens,
and you waters above the heavens!
Let them praise the name of the LORD,
for He commanded and they were created.

PSALM 148:3-5

❧

Lord, Your name is written on all Your works. Everything You created shouts with loudest praises what a wonderful God You are.

As I look at the immensity of Your creation, I see Your greatness. As I consider the complexity of Your works, I see Your wisdom. As I admire their beauty and usefulness, I realize Your goodness. And when I am reminded that You made them all from nothing, I am awed by Your power.

I am especially amazed when I remember that Your greatness, wisdom, goodness, and power have no beginning and no end. May I proclaim Your majesty with the same enthusiasm as all nature does!

The Crowning Glory of Creation

All Your works shall praise You, O Lord,
and Your saints shall bless You.

Psalm 145:10

∽

God of wonders, every part of Your creation magnifies Your greatness. Every creature in the earth, sea, and sky displays the beauty of Your handiwork. Every mountain, ocean, planet, and star proclaims the enormity of Your power. And yet when You created man and woman, You went above and beyond—You made them in Your very own image.

I am filled with awe that You chose to make humankind the crowning glory of Your creation. You gave us a special worth; we alone can know You in a personal and meaningful way. And even when we fell into sin, You chose to send a Redeemer and save us...showing how so very much You love us.

You alone, O Lord, are worthy of all praise!

God's Providence

Praise to the Lord, who o'er all things so wondrously reigneth,
Shelters thee under His wings, yea, so gently sustaineth!
Hast thou not seen How thy desires e'er have been
Granted in what He ordaineth!

JOACHIM NEANDER
"PRAISE TO THE LORD, THE ALMIGHTY"

The Source of True Riches

*Blessed be the God and Father of our Lord Jesus
Christ, who according to His abundant mercy has
begotten us…to an inheritance incorruptible and
undefiled and that does not fade away, reserved in
heaven for you.…*

1 PETER 1:3-4

∽

Lord, how I wish I were not so easily seduced by
the glittering attractions of this world. All too often I am
drawn to the empty treasures of this earth rather than
the satisfying riches of Your grace. You have given to me
the everlasting wealth of spiritual life and Your future
kingdom…and yet still I pursue contentment from that
which will one day turn to dust.

Oh, that I would take greater delight in hiding Your
Word in my heart, communing with You all day long,
and appreciating Your blessings in my life. May I seek
fulfillment in loving, serving, and praising You. Help me
to let go of the insignificant so that my hands and heart
are free to cling instead to that which is significant.

I praise You, Lord, for all the riches I possess in
You.

All Things Are Possible

I can do all things through Christ who strengthens me.

PHILIPPIANS 4:13

∽

Lord Jesus, I thank You that You don't expect me to live the Christian life in my own power. I admit that in my human weakness, obeying Your more difficult commands is hard. You say, "Love your enemies…do good to those who hate you, and pray for those who…persecute you" (Matthew 5:44). Lord, that's *very* hard to do!

Yet You also say, "Abide in me" so that You may enable me (John 15:4). You say, "Walk in the Spirit" so that I may bear the Spirit's fruit (Galatians 5:16,22-23). And You say to let Your Word dwell in me richly so that it may transform me (Colossians 3:16).

Yes, I *can* do all things because of the resources You've given me. All You ask is that I be an open and willing vessel. Thank You for Your provision!

We Have Everything

His divine power has given to us all things that pertain to life and godliness.

2 PETER 1:3

∽

Father, You have given me *everything* I need for life and godliness. You have given me...

Your Son Jesus, who made my salvation possible. He is also the vine that enables me, the branch, to bear fruit. As the apostle Paul said, I am *complete* in Christ (Colossians 2:10).

Your Holy Spirit, who is my Counselor and Comforter. Thank You for the promise that the Spirit will guide me in *all* truth (John 16:13).

And Your Word, which guides and corrects me so that I "may be thoroughly equipped for *every* good work" (2 Timothy 3:16-17 NIV).

In You, Father, I lack nothing. Thank You for giving so abundantly to me!

His Perfect Timing

Though the LORD is on high,
yet He regards the lowly....

PSALM 138:6

∽

Lord, I am awed as I consider that You stand above time. You can see all of eternity past and eternity future simultaneously. Time does not hem You in; rather, You are its master. You coordinate everything that happens on this earth according to Your perfect will. Nothing ever takes place too early or too late.

As I journey through the Bible, I see again and again how You cared for Your people in their moments of need, always at the right time. May that bring confidence to my heart whenever I become anxious about the future. Help me to rest and wait for Your provision...which I know will come at the perfect time. I have no need to worry about tomorrow, for You are already there.

Thank You, Lord

In everything give thanks....
1 Thessalonians 5:18

✑

Father, help me to realize the power of having a thankful heart. When I am grateful for what I have, Satan cannot sow the seeds of discontent in me.

When I am dissatisfied with my place in life, remind me to be grateful that I am even alive. When I complain about my responsibilities, stir me to gratitude that I was entrusted with them. When I resent others needing my help, cause me to be thankful that I can bring blessing into their lives.

May my every negative attitude, Lord, become positive through thankfulness to You. Teach me to truly give thanks in *everything,* for I know gratitude makes the difference between discouragement and joy.

God's Answers to Prayer

O Lord, in looking back we are obliged to remember
with the greatest gratitude the many occasions
in which Thou hast heard our cry.
We have been brought into deep distress,
and our heart has sunk within us,
and then have we cried to Thee and
Thou has never refused to hear us.[7]

CHARLES HADDON SPURGEON

He Hears Our Every Cry

Give ear to my words, O LORD,
consider my meditation.
Give heed to the voice of my cry,
my King and my God,
for to You I will pray.

PSALM 5:1-2

∞

Lord, thank You that You are always ready to hear my voice. Thank You for the psalmist's affirmation that I really am important to You. I don't need to beg You to hear me, for You *promise* to hear me!

And You hear not only my prayers but also those cries and anxieties that I cannot express. The assurance that You hear and understand me at all times brings great comfort and calm to my heart.

And Father, when I pray, may I be as willing to hear Your voice as You are to hear mine. May I listen to Your words to me in the Scriptures. May I seek, at all times, to accept the way You answer my prayers.

He Will Answer

In the day of my trouble I will call upon You,
for You will answer me.

PSALM 86:7

∽

Heavenly Father, when I am tossed to and fro by life's difficulties, I tend to allow fear and doubt to fill my mind. But when the storms pass and the sunshine returns, I look back in hindsight and can see clear evidence of Your guiding hand upon my life.

I see Your *incredible wisdom* in the way You allowed me to grow through the experience. I see Your *unceasing compassion* in the way You preserved me and brought help. I see Your *unfailing love* in the good that came out of the bad.

When I cry out to You, O Lord, I know You will answer. Your response may not be immediate, but I know it will come. I praise You for Your faithfulness to me in the past, and I know Your faithfulness to me will continue into the future.

The Lord Jesus Christ

All hail the power of Jesus' name!
Let angels prostrate fall;
Bring forth the royal diadem
And crown Him Lord of all!
Bring forth the royal diadem
And crown Him Lord of all!

Let every kindred, every tribe,
On this terrestrial ball,
To Him all majesty ascribe,
And crown Him Lord of all!
To Him all majesty ascribe,
And crown Him Lord of all!

EDWARD PERRONET
"ALL HAIL THE POWER OF JESUS' NAME"

With a Grateful Heart

Thanks be to God for His indescribable gift!

2 CORINTHIANS 9:15

∽

Father, *nothing* is more wonderful than what Jesus did for me at the cross. As the song proclaims, "Amazing love! How can it be that Thou my God shouldst die for me?"

I marvel as I consider the high price You paid so I could become Your child. You could have given up on me as hopelessly lost, but You didn't. Out of Your great love, for reasons I cannot explain, You chose to rescue me from the inescapable shackles of sin.

The suffering that Jesus endured on my behalf causes me to bow my head in quiet gratitude. I lift up my heart to You in worship…and may I *always* be filled with wonder because of the magnitude of Your love and grace!

The Beauty of His Humility

Jesus, who, being in the form of God...made Himself
of no reputation, taking the form of a bondservant....

PHILIPPIANS 2:5-6

∽

Jesus, though You are King of kings and Lord of lords and You are worthy of the highest honor and praise, You did not cling to Your position and Your glory when the time came to redeem humanity.

You did not consider Yourself too great to become a bondservant and grow up in poverty. You were not too proud to touch the untouchables and love the unlovable. You were not too significant to teach uneducated fishermen and ride on a donkey. No person was unimportant to You, no child was too small for You, no task was too menial. The sacrifices You made in Your life were many—even to the point of death!

Lord, You humbled Yourself that I might be exalted. May Your humility inspire me...and may I never consider myself too great to do the little things You have called me to do.

What a Savior!

*In Christ Jesus you who once were far off
have been brought near by the blood of Christ.*

EPHESIANS 2:13

∽

Jesus, I bow before You in silent adoration as I consider what You have done for me. You have rescued me from death. Cleansed me of sin. Lifted me from shame. Freed me from guilt. Raised me to life. Filled me with hope. Clothed me with righteousness. Calmed me with peace. Upheld me with strength. And secured me for heaven.

How can I express my gratitude to You? By glorying in Your cross. Resting in Your grace. Following in Your steps. Listening to Your words. Trusting in Your provision. Relying on Your faithfulness. Marveling in Your love. And rejoicing in Your promise of eternity with You.

Praising Christ for All Eternity

Worthy is the Lamb who was slain
to receive power and riches and wisdom,
and strength and honor and glory and blessing!

REVELATION 5:12

∾

Yes, Jesus, You are worthy of honor and glory! My every hope, my every blessing in life is possible because of You alone. Without Your sacrifice on the cross, I would have nothing. Because of Your precious blood shed at Calvary, I have everything.

Whatever praises come my way, may I pass them along to You. Whatever benefits I enjoy in life, remind me to thank You. Whatever rewards and crowns I gain here on earth, may I cast them at Your feet in heaven.

Regardless of how much honor and glory I give You, Jesus, I know I can always give more. For that reason I look forward to praising You for all eternity!

The Price of Redemption

*Father, I desire that they also whom You gave Me
may be with Me where I am....*

JOHN 17:24

∽

Lord, I am deeply moved by Your declaration that
You desired for me to live with You in heaven. Even before
I was born You determined to make me Yours, and You
put into action a plan that stopped at nothing to free me
from the clutches of sin.

You knew before You came to earth that You would be
persecuted and reviled. Hated and despised. Condemned
and crucified. You counted the cost...and still You desired
me. You paid much too high a price for me, and You did
it willingly.

Whenever I struggle over the cost of being Your child
in this hostile world, remind me, O Lord, that it is but a
small cost that I should gladly bear.

His Goodness Never Ends

*Blessed be the God and Father of our Lord Jesus
Christ, who according to His abundant mercy has
begotten us again to a living hope...to an inheritance incorruptible....*

1 PETER 1:3-4

∽

I praise You, Father, that because of the cross, the slate of my life has been wiped clean. No sin—past, present, or future—can be held against me. You paid the penalty in full, once and for all.

And Your Son did not stop with salvation. I know "He always lives to make intercession" for me (Hebrews 7:25). He watches over and sanctifies and cleanses me so that I might "be holy and without blemish" (Ephesians 5:27).

And there's still more! I will one day rule with Him in glory and enjoy "every spiritual blessing in the heavenly places" (Ephesians 1:3). What a gift You have given me in Jesus—Your goodness to me never ends!

Fairest Lord Jesus

*Walk in love, as Christ also has loved us
and given Himself for us....*

EPHESIANS 5:2

∽

I praise You, Lord Jesus, for the glorious example You are to me. From You I have learned how to love others with a tender compassion. You were not ashamed to be a friend to sinners or to offer a caring hand to the outcast. You gave comfort to the hurting and hope to the oppressed. With firmness You rebuked Your enemies, yet You did not take vengeance on them.

You came to serve, not to be served. You humbled Yourself to do the Father's will and not Your own. You endured great suffering with patience and fortitude. And You demonstrated that there is no greater love than to lay down one's life for others.

Thank You, dear Lord, for showing me how to live and to serve. May I be a willing follower in Your footsteps.

Responding to His Love

To Him who loved us and washed us from our sins in His own blood, and has made us kings and priests to His God and Father, to Him be glory and dominion forever and ever. Amen.

REVELATION 1:5-6

∽

Jesus, as I reflect on the wondrous display of Your love at the cross, my heart wells up in a gratitude too deep for words. You endured the worst of mortal suffering so that I might experience the best of immortal blessing. Because You submitted to the wrath and fury of Your Father, I am able to know the blessing and glory of Your Father.

At the outpouring of such love I cannot help but be moved. Oh, that I would be more devoted to You and follow You more wholeheartedly! Should temptation knock at the door of my heart, may I spurn it, for to sin would be inconsistent with the love I owe to You. Instead, may everything I say and do be worthy of being lifted up as an offering of thanksgiving and praise to You.

Love's Redeeming Work Is Done

But God raised Him up again, putting an end to the agony of death, since it was impossible for Him to be held in its power.

ACTS 2:24 NASB

∼

Father, how glorious are the words, "He is risen!" I magnify and praise You for Jesus' victory over the grave. With His resurrection, death reigns no more. And because He arose, I too will one day rise. Yes, love's redeeming work is done!

Today Jesus sits at Your right hand, highly exalted "far above all rule and authority, power and dominion" (Ephesians 1:21 NIV). Having died to save me, He now lives to make me holy and to prepare a place for me in heaven. Yes, Christ has opened paradise!

And a day is coming when every knee will bow, and every tongue will confess that Jesus Christ is Lord. He will reign over a new heaven and earth, and I will reign with Him—for all eternity. Yes, I will raise my joys and triumphs high!

The Holy Spirit

Come, holy Comforter,
Thy sacred witness bear
In this glad hour:
Thou who almighty art,
Now rule in every heart,
And ne'er from us depart,
Spirit of power.

ANONYMOUS
"COME, THOU ALMIGHTY KING"

The Ultimate Prayer Partner

*The Spirit also helps in our weaknesses. For we do
not know what we should pray for as we ought, but
the Spirit Himself makes intercession for us with
groanings which cannot be uttered.*

ROMANS 8:26

&

I exalt You, Lord, for the marvelous work of the
Holy Spirit on my behalf. In my human weaknesses and
limitations, I realize I do not always pray as I should.
Sometimes I don't know Your will for me. Sometimes I am
not aware of my true spiritual need. And sometimes I let
my human desires get in the way of Your divine plan.

Though I may pray with all sincerity, I realize my
requests are flawed at best. And so Your Holy Spirit steps
in and specifies my real needs in accord with His perfect
wisdom and Your perfect will. He says what I am unable
to say. I praise You for giving me such an Advocate—One
who will never cease to sustain and protect me. How
wonderful that You, the Son, and the Spirit are united in
caring for me in more ways than I'll ever know!

Honoring the Guest of Honor

I will pray the Father, and He will give you another Helper, that He may abide with you forever—the Spirit of truth....

JOHN 14:16-17

⌗

Lord, I find it incredible to know that at the moment of my salvation, Your Holy Spirit came to dwell in me. Your Spirit actually *lives* within me...so that He might enable me to live out my new identity as Your child. Yet at times I forget about His presence, and I grieve or ignore Him. At times He has to nudge my heart repeatedly before I listen to Him.

Dear Holy Spirit, I thank You for Your persistence. Jesus promised You would be my Advocate...and true to His word, You have been my unfailing help. You have guided and sustained me and made Christ real within me. May I always treat You as the Guest of Honor in my life by surrendering my all to receive Your all. Thank You, Holy Spirit, for abiding in me and helping me.

The Spirit's Love for Us

*You were sealed with the Holy Spirit of promise,
who is the guarantee of our inheritance....*

EPHESIANS 1:13-14

∽

Dear Holy Spirit, You show Your love for me in so many ways! You began by convicting me of my sin and my need for a Savior. At the moment of my salvation You sealed me for eternity, placed me in the body of Christ, and gave me spiritual gifts. You have given me new eyes to reveal the truths of Scripture to me. You dwell in me, pray for me, teach me, bear fruit through me, and are transforming me. And You are preserving me till that glorious day when my mortal body takes on immortality.

Thank You, Holy Spirit, for the many and constant expressions of Your love for me. Thank You for Your unceasing faithfulness.

Our Helper Who Enables Us

*When the Helper comes, whom I shall send to you
from the Father...He will testify of Me.*

JOHN 15:26

❧

Jesus, what a wonderful Helper the Holy Spirit is! He illumines the Scriptures for me so that I might understand them, and He points my attention to You so that I might learn from and become more like You.

Without the Spirit's light, I would be blind to You and Your truth. And without the Spirit's power, I would be unable to bear His fruit. He enables me to become all that You desire for me to be.

Because of Your Spirit, Lord, I can live victoriously. Thank You for sending Him into my life to dwell within me. May I always walk in Him and yield myself to His filling so that through me, others may see You too.

MAR. 12, Thurs. 10:00 A.M. PCH

110

The Bible

The Scripture is the standard of truth, the judge of controversies;
it is the pole-star to direct us to heaven....The Scripture is
the compass by which the rudder of our will is to be steered;
it is the field in which Christ, the Pearl of price, is hid;
it is a rock of diamonds; it is a sacred "eye-salve";
it heals their eyes that look upon it; it is a spiritual optic-glass
in which the glory of God is resplendent;
it is the panacea or "universal medicine" for the soul.[8]

THOMAS WATSON

A Purifying Power

Your word is very pure;
therefore Your servant loves it.

PSALM 119:140

∽

Father, the psalmist tells me Your Word is "*very* pure." It's pure to the point of perfection. That which You have said and written has no fault…no error…no sin. Rather, Your Word is pure in its influence…its wisdom…its counsel. And the more I expose myself to it, the more it washes and cleanses and purges me so that I may become a vessel fit for Your use.

May I delight in, honor, and hunger for Your Word. May I not only know it and cherish it but also practice it. May my obedience to its precepts be so complete that it shapes my every thought, word, and action. May I give myself wholly to Your Word so that it may wholly transform me.

The Perfect Guide

*Your word is a lamp to my feet
and a light to my path.*

PSALM 119:105

∽

Heavenly Father, Your living Word is so very precious
to me. All the treasures of the earth cannot purchase
for me that which I can receive from Your Word. Only
Scripture can convert the soul, make wise the simple,
rejoice the heart, enlighten the eyes, warn the heart, and
bring eternal reward (Psalm 19:7-8,11). Only Scripture can
make me truly complete in the way You intended, giving
me instruction and correction that prepares me for every
good work (2 Timothy 3:16).

Your Word, Lord, provides counsel for my every need.
May I always hunger and thirst for it; may I never tire of
mining its riches. What a mighty gift and guide You have
given me for all of life!

His Word a Source of Blessing

Your testimonies I have taken as a heritage forever,
for they are the rejoicing of my heart.

PSALM 119:111

∽

I praise You, Lord, that You are a God who desires to communicate with me. Your infinite wisdom and Your perfect will are made available to me at all times in Your beloved Word.

Through the Scriptures I can get to know You intimately...and I can listen as You speak to my heart. I can look back at how You guided and cared for Your children in ages past, knowing that You will provide the same guidance and care for me today. And Your Word is filled to overflowing with truths and promises that, when stored in my heart, are able to encourage and direct me at any moment of the day.

Father, I could never exhaust the treasure You have given me in Your Word. What a source of blessing it is to me!

In Times of Suffering

Fear not, I am with thee; O be not dismayed,
For I am thy God, and will still give thee aid;
I'll strengthen thee, help thee, and cause thee to stand,
Upheld by my righteous omnipotent hand.

ANONYMOUS
"HOW FIRM A FOUNDATION"

His Care Is Constant

…casting all your care upon Him, for He cares for you.

1 PETER 5:7

∾

Dear Father, You lovingly command me to surrender my cares to You. Too often I let the weight of my burdens press me down. Help me to remember that the heaviness on my mind and heart is not heaviness to You at all.

I praise You for Your promise to care for me in every season of life, regardless of how difficult. Though I may not see Your face, I know You are with me even in the darkest of night. Though I may not feel Your presence, I know You are always with me, a very present help in times of trouble.

Too often I see Your loving care only in that which is miraculous or obvious. Help me to see the many quiet and ordinary ways You care for me. Open my eyes to the constant expressions of Your love for me!

Always for Our Best

Count it all joy when you fall into various trials,
knowing that the testing of your faith produces
patience....that you may be perfect and complete,
lacking nothing.

JAMES 1:2-4

∽

Heavenly Father, I know You are too wise to ever make a mistake. When something appears to go wrong for me, I know it's not a mere accident.

Regardless of what sufferings I face, I know You have permitted them. Though I may not understand Your plan, help me to rest assured that You know which path I need to walk so I can become everything You desire for me to be. May I not seek to escape Your refining process; rather, may I allow Your purpose in my trial to be accomplished.

I praise You, Lord, that the testing of my faith helps me to grow stronger. Help me to always look ahead to the end result, knowing that even the worst of circumstances can turn out for my best.

The One We Can Count On

…sorrowful, yet always rejoicing….

2 CORINTHIANS 6:10

✍

Dear Lord, thank You for the apostle Paul's loving reminder that even in the midst of sorrow, I can continue to rejoice. Even when life is hard, I can know a deep inner joy…all because of the spiritual blessings You've given to me, which can never be taken away.

Even when life goes wrong, You are a Shepherd who will care for me, a Friend who will stay with me, a Father who will watch over me. You are a Rock who will help me stand firm, a Shield who will protect me from danger, a Counselor who will guide me.

When all else seems lost, I know I can still count on You. Even when I can't think of anything to be thankful for, in reality, I have much to be thankful for. I praise You, Lord, for Your faithfulness to me.

From Despair to Praise

Why are you cast down, O my soul?
And why are you disquieted within me?
Hope in God, for I shall yet praise Him.

PSALM 42:5

∽

Father, too often I come to You grumbling and complaining rather than worshiping and adoring. I can so easily become preoccupied with the ugliness of my circumstances and forget that You have the wisdom and power to create something good and beautiful out of them all.

When my focus is negative, nudge my heart…and remind me to dwell on that which is true, noble, just, pure, lovely, of good report, virtuous, and praiseworthy (Philippians 4:8). Though I may not be able to change that which is around me, I know You can change my heart and my perspective. May I learn the calming hope and peace that comes from praising You even when I don't feel like it.

The Healer of Our Hurts

Out of the depths I have cried to You, O LORD;
Lord, hear my voice!
Let Your ears be attentive
to the voice of my supplications.

PSALM 130:1-2

∽

Lord, You know the hidden sighs of my heart. You know my secret anguish, my silent tears. Your all-seeing eyes perceive the suffering that no one else sees. Though I may hide my grief from those around me, I can hide nothing from You...and for that, I am grateful.

Others may abandon me, but You are always near. Others may misunderstand me, but You don't. Even my own heart deceives me at times, but You will never betray me.

Because You are all-knowing, You alone can comfort and heal me. You alone can guide and restore me. Regardless of the cause of my hurt, You know the way to help me. You are indeed the Great Physician!

Persevering and Praising

Christ also suffered for us, leaving us an example,
that you should follow His steps.

1 PETER 2:21

∽

Dear Lord, You have called me to have a heart filled with rejoicing and praise. Yet in my human frailty, I am all too prone to grumbling and despair.

I thank You that Your Son has already walked the difficult road before me and given me a pattern I can follow. When my heart aches from life's burdens…when I am wounded by those around me…when I am persecuted for righteousness' sake…I need only to remember how Your Son was humiliated, afflicted, rejected, and despised. And through it all, He remained patient, loving, and steadfast—even to the point of death. By comparison, I have suffered little.

May my recollection of Jesus' faithfulness refresh me and give me new strength. Teach me to endure as Jesus did…and to praise You in all things at all times.

The Perspective from Eternity

*For of Him and through Him and to Him are all
things, to whom be glory forever. Amen.*

ROMANS 11:36

∽

Heavenly Father, there is so much of life that I don't
understand. You say that all things work together for good
to those who love You. Yet at times I feel so overwhelmed
by my problems that I can't help but ask…why me? And
for what purpose?

I thank You that someday, I will stand with You on
the hilltops of glory and look back at the landscape of my
life…and I will see more clearly how You used every rough
path I walked to polish me and make me more complete.
I will see what I didn't see before—that You permitted my
trials out of love, You enabled me to endure them, and
You used them to bring You honor.

May I not wait until then to praise You for Your
perfecting work in me. May I start praising You right
now…and trusting all the more Your great faithfulness.

In Times of Worship

O for a thousand tongues to sing
My great Redeemer's praise,
The glories of my God and King,
The triumphs of His grace.

My gracious Master and my God,
Assist me to proclaim,
To spread through all the earth abroad
The honors of Thy name.

CHARLES WESLEY
"O FOR A THOUSAND TONGUES"

The Power of Praise

Praise the LORD!
I will praise the LORD
with my whole heart.

PSALM 111:1

∽

Father, thank You for the gift of praise, which allows me to express my love and adoration to You. Thank You for the special way that praise enriches and elevates the relationship I enjoy with You.

My desire, Lord, is that my praise will always bring joy to You. Even when my heart is downcast...and even when times are hard...may my praise be whole and genuine. Even when I seem to have nothing to be thankful for, remind me that I have much to be grateful for.

Thank You for the way praise can lift my heart and help me view my circumstances in a new light. Thank You for how it can turn a worldly defeat into a spiritual victory!

No Greater Privilege

Serve the LORD with gladness;
come before His presence with singing.

PSALM 100:2

∽

Lord, what is the mood of my heart when I serve You? Am I serving You with gladness or because I have to? Is my service prompted by love or by duty?

Being Your servant is such a privilege! Nothing is ordinary about the work You have called me to. May I always be mindful of whom I serve…and may I find satisfaction in knowing that everything I do for You will bear fruit that lasts for eternity.

My service, O Lord, is but a drop compared to the ocean of blessings You've poured out on me. That is reason enough for me to always serve You with gladness and singing. May my service to You be so attractive that others are able to see more of Your greatness.

He Is Worthy of Praise…Always

I will praise You, O LORD, with my whole heart;
I will tell of all Your marvelous works.
I will be glad and rejoice in You;
I will sing praise to Your name, O Most High.

PSALM 9:1-2

∽

Lord, thank You for the example the psalmist provides in these words. Not once, not twice, but four times he says, "I will." What dedication, to make praise such a high priority!

Help me to praise You not only in the bright days of life but also in the dark nights. And may I give that praise with my whole heart. Though my circumstances may change, I know Your love for me is constant…and therefore my praise ought to be constant too.

From the psalmist I also learn that one way to praise You is to tell of all Your marvelous works. Father, may I always be alert to opportunities to speak of Your care in my life. How will others know of Your greatness unless I proclaim it?

Slow Down and Worship

My voice You shall hear in the morning, O LORD;
in the morning I will direct it to You, and I will look up.

PSALM 5:3

∽

Lord, convict me when I become too busy to praise You when I first wake up. Starting the day with You helps me view everything from Your heavenly perspective rather than my earthly one.

Help me to slow down and marvel over Your great power, which can perform wonders beyond what I can imagine...Your steadfast love, which cares for me regardless of what happens...and Your perfect knowledge, which anticipates my every need from today into eternity.

Remembering how awesome You are makes such a difference! Then I can face the day with boldness rather than fear...peace rather than anxiety...and hope rather than despair.

Glorifying Him
Through Our Praise

Whoever offers praise glorifies Me.

PSALM 50:23

∽

Lord, help me to remember at all times that my life is a stage on which other people can see You on display. Each time I share with others how You've blessed me, I am giving them a glimpse of Your greatness. Each time I praise You, I am bringing honor to You.

And Lord, You are so worthy of that honor! You have blessed me far beyond what I deserve. You have raised me up in Christ and given me a spiritual inheritance that will never perish. You have surrounded me with people who care about me. And You have provided for my every need.

As I recount each of Your blessings, Lord, may I declare them to others and bring glory to You.

Celebrating the Gift of Praise

Oh, that men would give thanks to the LORD for His goodness....
For He satisfies the longing soul....

PSALM 107:8-9

∽

Lord, I thank You for gifting me with the ability to know and worship You. I am so blessed to be able to converse with You and exalt You. As I lift up my prayers and gratitude to You, I feel my heart lifted up as well.

When I bow before Your throne in adoration, I sense within me a satisfaction unlike any other. As I magnify Your name, I experience true happiness and contentment.

Thank You for allowing me the privilege of offering up praises to You. May I grow to cherish this privilege and let it permeate every part of my life. I will never have enough days to celebrate Your greatness—not even in eternity!

The Hope of Heaven

When we've been there ten thousand years
Bright shining as the sun,
We've no less days to sing God's praise
Than when we'd first begun.

JOHN NEWTON
"AMAZING GRACE"

Created for Eternity

God, who is rich in mercy...made us alive together
with Christ...that in the ages to come He might
show the exceeding riches of His grace....

EPHESIANS 2:4-7

∽

Heavenly Father, as a creature of this earth, I can easily get caught up in that which is fleeting and temporary. Remind me that my time here is short and that You have redeemed me for eternity. May I always be mindful that this world is not my home and that I am a citizen of a better world to come.

Help me to not limit my vision and my desires to the things that will perish. Teach me to set my mind on the exceeding riches of Your grace—"on things above, not on things on the earth" (Colossians 3:2). Fortify me to resist the temptations that will divert me from that which really counts. May my life *here* always be focused on *eternity!*

The Promise of His Return

When the Son of Man comes in His glory, and all the holy angels with Him, then He will sit on the throne of His glory.

MATTHEW 25:31

❧

Lord, how I love the promise of Your coming! In a world that increasingly rejects You and takes pleasure in wickedness, the assurance of Your return is a blessed hope to which I can hold fast.

In that glorious day, the world that was lost to sin will be won to righteousness. The creation that fell under bondage to corruption will be restored to its full beauty. And Your children will at long last be changed from mortality to immortality.

How I look forward to the time when You will triumph once and for all over sin, pain, hatred, and injustice…and You will rule from Your throne with all glory, power, majesty, and authority!

Living in Anticipation of Heaven

We, according to His promise, look for new heavens and a new earth in which righteousness dwells.

2 PETER 3:13

℘

Father, time and again Your Word reminds me that I am merely a pilgrim here on earth and that my real home is heaven. You urge me to set my affections on the glories above and not the things of earth.

And no wonder! The treasures of earth are but dull trinkets compared to the brilliant jewels of heaven. The happiness and love and contentment I know here are but a faint image of what I will know in my celestial home.

Thank You, Father, for the promise of heaven. In the times when I am weary, may I fix my heart upon the joys that await me in the realms of bliss…knowing that to do so will renew my strength and carry me onward in this journey called life.

The Joy of Heaven

In Your presence is fullness of joy;
at Your right hand are pleasures forevermore.

PSALM 16:11

∽

In Your presence, Lord, is a fullness of joy that will be more satisfying than any I can know here on earth. No more will I endure the wintry storms that cast darkness and hardship upon my path. No more will the havoc wrought by sin rob me of peace and rest.

And this joy will be everlasting—one that will never end. No more will sin ever interrupt my fellowship with You. No more will I ever have to depart from the presence of loved ones and dear saints. No more will I ever live in fear of sorrow, pain, and death.

Lead me through the wilderness, Lord, to the safety of heaven's shores. And along the way, spur me onward with Your promise that "weeping may endure for a night, but joy comes in the morning" (Psalm 30:5).

Destined for Glory

We know that when He is revealed, we shall be like Him, for we shall see Him as He is.

1 JOHN 3:2

❧

Father, on many days I feel like anything but a child of God. I entertain thoughts not pleasing to You, I speak words unbecoming of You, and I carry out actions that bring reproach upon You.

And yet through it all, You still forgive me, keep me, and love me as Your child. With patience and tenderness You continue to refine me more and more into the image of Your Son—till that wonderful day when, at last, I shall be like Him.

I love You, Lord, for Your grace, which has destined me for glory. For Your guidance, which enables my progress. And for Your faithfulness, which will bring me home. You are my hope, my joy, my crown.

Praise God from whom all blessings flow,
Praise Him all creatures here below,
Praise Him above, ye heavenly host,
Praise Father, Son, and Holy Ghost.

THOMAS KEN

∞

DOXOLOGY,
FROM "AWAKE MY SOUL, AND WITH THE SUN"

Notes

1. A.W. Tozer, *The Knowledge of the Holy* (San Francisco: Harper & Row, 1961), p. 116.

2. A.W. Pink, *Gleanings in the Godhead* (Chicago: Moody Press, 1975), p. 47.

3. Stephen Charnock, *The Existence and Attributes of God*, vol. 2 (Grand Rapids: Baker Book House, 1996), p. 211.

4. John MacArthur, *The Love of God*, (Dallas: Word Publishing, 1969), p. 169.

5. Christopher Christian Sturm, *Morning Communings with God*, vol. 1 (London: Baldwin, Cradock, and Joy, 1825), p. 49.

6. A.W. Tozer, *The Knowledge of the Holy* (San Francisco: Harper & Row, 1961), p. 62.

7. Dinsdale Young, *C.H. Spurgeon's Prayers* (London: Passmore & Alabaster, 1905), p. 148.

8. Thomas Watson, *Puritan Sermons*, vol. 2 (Wheaton, IL: Richard Owen Roberts Publishing, 1981), pp. 62-64.